BROADWAY SONGS FOR TWO

Arrangements by Peter Deneff

ISBN 978-1-5400-1284-5

HAL•LEONARD®

7777 W. BLUEMOUND RD. P.O. BOX 13819 MILWAUKEE, WI 53213

CONTENTS

ANY DREAM WILL DO
from JOSEPH AND THE AMAZING TECHNICOLOR® DREAMCOAT

CLARINETS

Music by ANDREW LLOYD WEBBER
Lyrics by TIM RICE

BRING HIM HOME

from LES MISÉRABLES

CLARINETS

Music by CLAUDE-MICHEL SCHÖNBERG
Lyrics by HERBERT KRETZMER
and ALAIN BOUBLIL

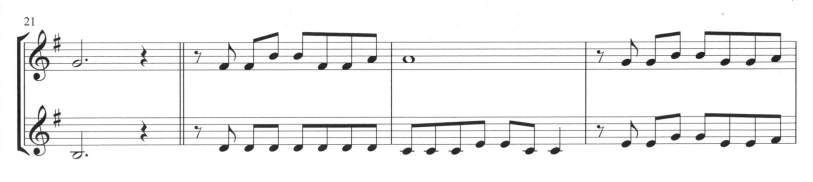

D.S. al Coda

CODA

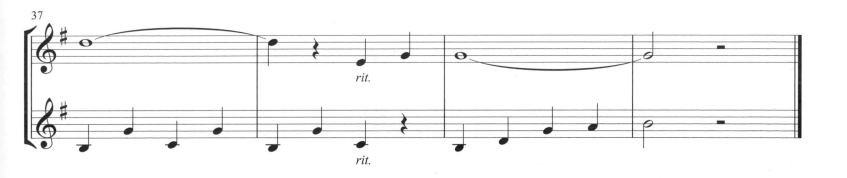

rit.

rit.

CABARET
from the Musical CABARET

CLARINETS

Words by FRED EBB
Music by JOHN KANDER

Moderately

EDELWEISS
from THE SOUND OF MUSIC

CLARINETS

Lyrics by OSCAR HAMMERSTEIN II
Music by RICHARD RODGERS

FOR FOREVER

from DEAR EVAN HANSEN

CLARINETS

Music and Lyrics by BENJ PASEK
and JUSTIN PAUL

HELLO, DOLLY!
from HELLO, DOLLY!

CLARINETS

Music and Lyric by
JERRY HERMAN

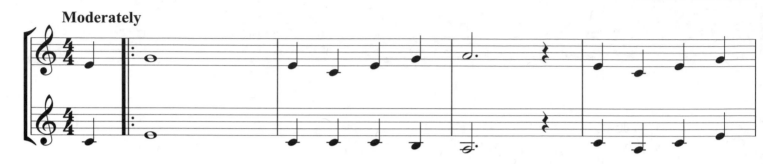

I BELIEVE

from the Broadway Musical THE BOOK OF MORMON

Clarinets

Words and Music by TREY PARKER,
ROBERT LOPEZ and MATT STONE

I WHISTLE A HAPPY TUNE

from THE KING AND I

CLARINETS

Lyrics by OSCAR HAMMERSTEIN II
Music by RICHARD RODGERS

IF I WERE A BELL
from GUYS AND DOLLS

CLARINETS

By FRANK LOESSER

THE IMPOSSIBLE DREAM
(The Quest)
from MAN OF LA MANCHA

CLARINETS

Lyric by JOE DARION
Music by MITCH LEIGH

MAMMA MIA

from MAMMA MIA!

CLARINETS

Words and Music by BENNY ANDERSSON,
BJÖRN ULVAEUS and STIG ANDERSON

MEMORY
from CATS

CLARINETS

Music by ANDREW LLOYD WEBBER
Text by TREVOR NUNN after T.S. ELIOT

Slowly, with feeling

MY FAVORITE THINGS
from THE SOUND OF MUSIC

CLARINETS

Lyrics by OSCAR HAMMERSTEIN II
Music by RICHARD RODGERS

ONE

from A CHORUS LINE

CLARINETS

Music by MARVIN HAMLISCH
Lyric by EDWARD KLEBAN

POPULAR
from the Broadway Musical WICKED

CLARINETS

Music and Lyrics by
STEPHEN SCHWARTZ

SEASONS OF LOVE

from RENT

CLARINETS

Words and Music by
JONATHAN LARSON

Moderately

SEVENTY SIX TROMBONES

from Meredith Willson's THE MUSIC MAN

CLARINETS

By MEREDITH WILLSON

SUMMERTIME
from PORGY AND BESS®

CLARINETS

Music and Lyrics by GEORGE GERSHWIN,
DuBOSE and DOROTHY HEYWARD
and IRA GERSHWIN

SUNRISE, SUNSET

from the Musical FIDDLER ON THE ROOF

CLARINETS

Words by SHELDON HARNICK
Music by JERRY BOCK

TOMORROW

from the Musical Production ANNIE

CLARINETS

Lyric by MARTIN CHARNIN
Music by CHARLES STROUSE

WHERE IS LOVE?

from the Broadway Musical OLIVER!

CLARINETS

Words and Music by
LIONEL BART

Slowly, tenderly

YOU'VE GOT A FRIEND

featured in BEAUTIFUL: THE CAROLE KING MUSICAL

CLARINETS

Words and Music by
CAROLE KING

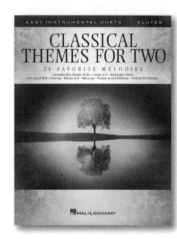